NO LONGER HIDDEN

LaTasha S. Lee

Copyright © 2022 LaTasha S. Lee

Scripture quotations marked "KJV" are taken from the Holy Bible, King James Version (Public Domain). Scripture quotations marked (NIV) are taken from the Holy Bible, New International Version®, NIV®. Copyright © 1973, 1978, 1984 by Biblica, Inc.™ Used by permission of Zondervan. All rights reserved worldwide. Scripture quotations marked "NKJV" are taken from the New King James Version. Copyright © 1982 by Thomas Nelson, Inc. Used by permission. All rights reserved. Bible text from the New King James Version® is not to be reproduced in copies or otherwise by any means except as permitted in writing by Thomas Nelson, Inc., Attn: Bible Rights and Permissions. No part of this document may be reproduced or transmitted in any form or by any means, electronic, mechanical, photocopying, recording, or otherwise, without prior written permission of the author.

NO LONGER HIDDEN

LaTasha S. Lee
latashalee7723@gmail.com

ISBN 978-1-949826-35-7

Printed in the USA.
All rights reserved

Published by: EAGLES GLOBAL BOOKS | Frisco, Texas
In conjunction with the 2022 Eagles Authors Course
Cover & interior designed by DestinedToPublish.com

DEDICATION

I dedicate this book to my mom, Carolyn Lee, who was always there for me. My cheerleader who always had my back, even when I didn't know she was interceding on my behalf. Thank you for your support and always believing in me. In my darkest state, you continued to pray and trust God, and now ALL can see the manifestation of what God has done. I also want to dedicate this book to every person who opens it. I pray that as you read this book, the shackles will be destroyed, and you will be set free in Jesus' name. I also want to dedicate this book to that special little girl who holds a very special place in my heart. I'll see you on the other side in glory.

ACKNOWLEDGMENTS

I first want to give glory and honor to my Lord and Savior Jesus Christ, who has given me strength to write this book. I want to also thank my parents, Allen Lee Sr. and Carolyn Lee, for all their prayers, support, and just being there during the most difficult transition I have ever faced. I thank God for my siblings, Dekisha Lee, Jamie Lee, and Allen Lee II, who kept me encouraged. I want to give a very special tribute to all my aunts and uncles. Lastly, I would like to thank the army that God sent to intercede on my behalf: Lorraine Render, Sharon Perkins, Charlene Johnson, Sharon Price, Jikhara Williams, Dorothy Matthews, Pastor Ron and Lady Ruth, Pastor Mitchel, and my JBS family (Spring cohort of 2021).

FOREWORD
by Lorraine Render

This book is a must-read for everyone, whether you know Christ as your personal Savior or you don't know if God is real. If you are a Christian, this book will challenge you to seek God for yourself. If you are not a believer, it will challenge you to seek God for yourself.

The author is someone I know is telling the truth. She lived this, and it is not fiction. LaTasha's experiences warn us to be aware that not everyone who says "Lord, Lord" is following Jesus. Charlatans and thieves can quote scriptures, but they can't live the out the Word of God, because the Word of God is truth.

If you don't believe in God or you don't know if God is real, you must read this book. God is real. God's Word is true. God created you for His purpose. You can only know what your purpose is when, like LaTasha, you are no longer hidden in an existence designed to keep you in bondage instead of letting you live the truth.

No Longer Hidden

Contents

Introduction 1

Chapter 1:
Separated for Purpose 3

Chapter 2:
No Longer Muted 13

Chapter 3:
Unleash Yourself 23

Chapter 4:
False Appearances 28

Chapter 5:
Learning to Walk in Wholeness through Faith 32

Chapter 6:
Standing Regardless of What Is Seen or Felt 43

Chapter 7:
Fighting Wrongful Thinking 48

Chapter 8:
Recognizing the Enemy 55

Chapter 9:
Walking in Freedom and Free from Religion 59

Chapter 10:
Delicate Yet Unbreakable 64

Chapter 11:
The Season Was Necessary 69

References 83

INTRODUCTION

The purpose of this book is to help others recognize that their journey ends in victory with Christ. No matter what you have been through in life, regardless of any pain you have experienced, God has a plan. No matter what tries to come your way, know that God is love and there is no condemnation in Christ. He has given us a free will, so don't allow religion to keep you in bondage. We must know who we are in Christ, for many are in bondage due to a lack of knowledge. The enemy will try to present things within your mind, but if you trust God and declare his word by speaking it out of your mouth you will have what you say. What you may have thought was impossible, God can and will manifest according to your faith, because nothing is impossible with Christ. One day, that manifestation will display not only the love of God, but a testimony for his glory.

God loves us and wants us to live in wholeness. He wants us to be happy. He wants us to be free. Wholeness is the entire package, because there is nothing missing or broken within wholeness. We don't have to live in condemnation due to what others say. When you sense fear, know that it is not of God, but of satan, for God has not given us the spirit of fear. God has given us our own will, and he does not interfere with our will. Therefore, if someone tries to take your will and make you submit to their will, know that it is not from God. Many in the church are living in condemnation due to what is falsely taught. I was one who gave up my will. Ouch! And it did actually hurt emotionally, physically and spiritually. I tried to live for God in all I knew how, but I was doing it the wrong way. Pleasing others is not pleasing God. I loved so hard that I overlooked the one who is LOVE (Christ). I am sharing my story so that you don't go down the path I went down. Get to know God for yourself and know that he will not leave you or forsake you.

– CHAPTER 1 –

Separated for Purpose

From day one, I was separated. My mom delivered me in a hospital all alone. Mom was a teen when she found out she was pregnant with me. According to her, several people tried to convince her to abort me. Thank God she didn't. My mom says that a couple of hours after my birth, she heard me crying, and that was strange because there were many babies in the nursery. How did she recognize my cry?

According to my mom, she was so sleepy because she had been given a sedative to help her sleep. She staggered her way into the nursery area to find me, and the nurse stopped her, asking her why she was out of bed. She told the nurse that she heard me crying. The nurse asked how, when all these babies were in the nursery. They then told her that I was in a separate room because I had a fever, and they didn't know what was wrong. Later they found that the fever had developed due to jaundice. The nurse led her to the room I was in, which was the room directly across from her. God had me separated, knowing that I had a call on my life.

My mom ended up giving her life to Christ as her personal Savior at the age of nineteen even though she was brought up in church. All I can remember since childhood was going to church on Wednesdays, Fridays, and all day on Sundays. While going to church and trying to live for God wholeheartedly, I was still deceived and hurt. Nevertheless, I've learned that even though I was crushed, it didn't destroy me but produced beauty in what God was developing in and through me. We are precious jewels. When I think of a diamond, they are made underground with high temperatures and lots of pressure. That is how God had me: I thought I couldn't take the heat, but I survived. I thought I couldn't take the pressure, yet I have come out as a unique treasure piece that is designed for the Master's use.

Becoming a masterpiece is not an easy thing to achieve. Life presents so many paths, and you may think you are making the right selection, but with one wrong turn, you could end up in a wilderness so dark and deep wondering how you got there. These paths present so many directions that are not always understood, causing one to question, "Why me?" Some circumstances are a result of our own ignorance, consequences, or an unexpected situation that caught you off guard. However, disappointments, hardships, joy, sadness, and pain pave the paths every one of us will have to make. Each tear smudges the path we take, showing the difficulty we have faced, and each tear will create a unique, original design from your pain, which will make it only your story to proclaim.

No one can tell your story like you, even if they were there to see what you went through. The result will be well displayed and worthy of all the uncomfortable pain. Many will be wowed to witness the achiever you have become, but they will also know who it was that brought you through… which was God, and no one can deny that. It is not easy becoming this masterpiece that others admire so dearly without knowing the value of the process it took to get you there. Have faith in yourself when all the odds are against you. Think positive, especially when doubt and negativity surround you. Forgive those who have hurt you by taking the power from them and energizing yourself to become the best. I present this to encourage you by letting you know you are special to God, and he only wants your best despite the things you may face. So, when things try to get you down – and believe me, life will present those unexpected challenges too – just know that God will carry you through, but it's up to you.

Receiving Christ

I was raised in church and had a great foundation. I remember giving my life to Christ at the age of seven in Sunday school. My teacher's name was Sister Joyce Dixon. She began to explain how God loved us and the difference between heaven and hell. I was so excited about giving my life to Christ and what I had learned that I want my best friend, Maureen, who lived upstairs to receive Christ as her personal Savior as well. When I got home, I went to tell Maureen what I had learned in Sunday school, and we knelt to pray in the enclosed back porch. She prayed and asked Jesus to come into her life as well. That is how it should be done when telling others about Christ.

Growing up in church

I remember my mom having my siblings and me memorizing scriptures on a weekly basis, and we had to pray together every morning before leaving for school. As I got older, I didn't want to attend church anymore, and my mom would say, "If you live here, you are going to church." Of course, I began to rebel. Life itself began to happen at home, and there was pressure, especially when my dad began to do drugs and got deeper and deeper, causing the drugs to consume him. My siblings and I handled the situation much differently, as I poured myself into church while my sister and brother went in other directions to cope with what was going on at home. I had a praying mother who refused to give up or in. She stood on faith, declaring God's promises for salvation for her household and every need met. God answered those prayers by giving her the wisdom to keep the household running along with putting us through private school.

The beginning of my junior year of high school, I met a classmate, and we begin to talk about church. She invited me to her church, which was filled with lots of young people. I began to go to her church on Friday nights with her and eventually became a member. I even moved into the pastor's house to help the people of God, as they were fostering several disabled children. I was giving up everything to follow God, or so I thought. God's word is truth regardless of what it looks like, while facts and logic may seem to be true but are a lie if they don't line up with the word of God. Grace looks beyond what we have done in the past, and condemnation is what the enemy wants us to live in, which causes fear and a lack of understanding of one's worth in God. For God has not given us the spirit of fear, no matter what surrounds us. When you have done something displeasing to God and you ask for forgiveness, don't keep contemplating what you have done, but know that through grace, God loves you unconditionally. When God corrects, he does it in love, and anything else is not of God. Truth is knowledge that reflects the word of God, and logic reflects self-reasoning. The enemy wants us to justify things through our feelings, what is seen, and logic, which doesn't produce faith.

Accepting deception

I had a zeal to live a holy life for God, as I was willing to do everything to please him. However, I now realize I was not actually pleasing God, for I was doing things by works and pleasing man instead. I listened to what they said God's plan was for my life instead of asking God for myself. I literally surrendered my life and will to man without consulting God for myself. I was told that God sent me there just to help watch and keep a special-needs child who was adopted. Many times, I would ask myself if all God had for me to do was to babysit. I would then repent for questioning God and pray for some relief. Little did I know that I was really being deceived by the enemy due to a lack of knowledge, as I was seeking to obey God by listening to what man said I should do. The word of God says men perish for a lack of knowledge (Hosea 4:6). I was living in bondage, depressed, sick, and just existing as I was completing my daily routine with a mindset of slavery.

I thank God for the people who kept me up in prayer, even those I didn't even know. For God yet had a plan for me, and his plan was that I be free. As I began to discover the love of God and how much he cared for me, my mindset began to change. I once thought that I had to do everything right and that if I didn't, I would be punished, and some type of consequence would come upon me. One thing I've realized is that Jesus paid it all on Calvary. Do we really know what that means concerning what he paid on Calvary, as many are yet living in bondage and living under the law instead of grace? When I think of being under the law, it consists of a set of rules that must be followed and have an unpleasant consequence if broken. Meanwhile, grace is something that we don't deserve; we didn't earn it but have received it because of the love of God. When Jesus went to Calvary, he did it not because we deserved it but because of his love for us. Once we accept Jesus Christ as our personal Savior and have repented, our sins are forgiven, and because of grace, we have a newness in Christ.

You may be thinking you have no one to intercede for you, but that's not true: I am the intercessor that God has sent to intercede just for you. I pray that everyone who reads this book and is in bondage will find that the truth is being revealed and your eyes are opening so that you can plainly see. I pray for a way of escape for you. I pray that the shackles be loosed, and that every chain that holds you fall and be destroyed, for who God sets free is free indeed. And according to the word of God, *"You shall know the truth, and the truth shall make you free"* (John 8:32 NKJV).

Free from living under the law

Living under the law presents fear and causes you to try to make sure you are doing everything correctly, when you can't do anything at all without God. When we try to do things ourselves, we are operating in the flesh. I personally found myself trying to submit to leadership within the church more than I submitted unto the Lord. This was a big mistake, not asking God for myself. I just tried to do what leadership said I should do because they were the people of God. I even did this when I truly did not want to because of fear of being rebuked or hearing them say I wasn't obeying leadership and therefore wasn't obeying God.

The spirit of fear also muted me. I wouldn't speak up regarding my own opinions and my own desires, nor to say how I felt, due to being embarrassed and rebuked in front of others. It was said often that open rebuke was good for the soul. Therefore, I was suppressed from expressing my feelings, thoughts, and concerns. This is not of God, *"for God has not given us a spirit of fear, but of power and of love and of a sound mind"* (2 Timothy 1:7 NKJV). Anytime you feel fear, know it's from satan. I remember praying, asking God not to allow me to say anything wrong and to help me do things right so my day would be blessed. Now, as I look back, I see the shackles that had me bound. Yes, situations will occur, for we live here on earth, but no matter the circumstance, satan will try to present fear, doubt, and unbelief. We must know who we are and stand on God's word no matter what, for salvation does not have you in fear or in shackles, but at rest, knowing who you are in Christ.

The truth is God's word

God's word is the truth regardless of what it seems like in the natural. Satan wants us as believers to go by the way we see things with our natural eye: how we feel with our emotions, or how we view things through what other people think. Having truth means having knowledge that contains God's word. God's word is not relatable to what we think, feel, see, or hear. God's word stands against logic but stands with faith.

Altered facts are lies that are presented through the enemy. For example, a believer may say, "God, please heal me." Yes, God is a healer, and he wants us to walk in wholeness, being complete in him. However, the word of God says that by his stripes we were healed (Isaiah 53:5; 1 Peter 2:24). This statement uses the past tense, meaning that is has already been done and all we have to do is receive it, just as we did salvation. It may not have manifested within this realm as of yet, but it has already been done. I had to learn this as I prayed regarding having brain surgery. Yes, the symptoms were there, but I had to confess the word instead of what the images and doctors said. Satan tries to alter the word of God through the words that come out of our mouth, and most of the time, we don't recognize the defeat within our words because they relate with our flesh and senses.

False doctrine

Spiritual blindness produces false doctrine. That is why we must study the word of God for ourselves. Don't get me wrong, having a pastor is very important, as God has sent them to be our shepherds. However, they are human as well, and there are some pastors who weren't sent by God but went for alternative reasons. I do believe that there are some leaders who operate in tradition and are not led by the Spirit of God, for religion and its traditions can present non-truths. Many grew up in church believing certain things, only to have to relearn what they had been taught. These non-truths are dangerous, as satan tries to blind the believers to what they are entitled to through Christ. He doesn't want the believer to know their benefits because he is afraid, they will use their weapons against him. You see, he knows the power in the word of God, and he's aware that if you learn how to use the word of God, his plans against you won't succeed. Satan works in darkness, and he wants the church to be spiritually blind and believe doctrines that don't affect him or his kingdom.

– CHAPTER 2 –

No Longer Muted

Being muted means being silent or non-expressive. God has given us a voice along with free will. Once we become a believer, he tells us to become a witness for him. Therefore, satan wants us to be silent. He desires to shut us up. How can we talk about the goodness of Christ if we are shut up?

I have found myself muted even within the church. Fear had me muted as I became subject to leadership and other opinions, trying to please them regardless of how I felt. God has given us a free will, and we have the right to voice our opinions without being afraid of disappointing leadership. Now, I'm not saying to be disrespectful, but we have our own thoughts and personalities that are uniquely made by God. God does not go against your will, even if it does not line up with his. So, putting another person's will above your own just to please them is not of God. It's like having another god before him.

FEAR LEADS TO BONDAGE

Fear had me muted and afraid. When I spoke how I felt, I was rebuked or told I needed to be delivered. This caused me to get more in bondage as I suppressed my own will to comply with another man's will. We as God's people must be able to speak without being fearful of leadership within the church. Satan uses fear as a tactic to hold God's people in bondage, as well as to control them. I remember times in church where the pastor would state, "I hear what you are thinking, and if you don't stop it, I will call you out." I asked God, "Where in the Bible did this happen?" As I began to search God's word, I saw in 1 Corinthians 2:11 in the New International Version, *"For who knows a person's thoughts except their own spirit within them? In the same way no one knows the thoughts of God except the Spirit of God."* I believe this tactic was used also as a fear tool. If it's not in God's word, it's not the truth. When are we going to stop listening to what people say and listen to God's word instead? We must stop taking another person's word without finding a scripture to back it up. Again, if it's not in God's word, then it's not the truth, for many are deceived due to a lack of knowledge.

THE TRAP

The trap is out to catch you off guard. Now, if we think of a mouse trap, we see that something is connected or placed on the trap that the mouse desires, not realizing that it's there to cause them harm. It is a counterfeit: it looks real, but it isn't what God has for you, because God only has the best for you. God doesn't want to hurt you or trap you. If we recognize things by our senses (smell, touch, hear, sight, taste), we can believe the counterfeit. Therefore, we must be mindful and prayerful, for satan has also studied your life and knows your desires. One of his assignments is to keep you blind from the truth as he presents lies and fear.

JUNIOR YEAR

In the beginning of my junior year of high school, I became friends with a classmate, and she invited me to come to her church's Friday night service. I begged my mom because she was so overprotective with my siblings and me. After talking to an adult who attended the church, she then gave her permission for me to go. When I went to my friend's church, it was mostly young people, and it was so amazing to see so many young people who seemed to have a zeal for God. You see, at that time, being at home was rough because my dad had started using drugs. (Thank God he is now a believer and goes into prisons teaching the word of God and allowing God to use his experiences for his glory.) Going to church was an outlet as I could cry out to God. I ended up joining this church after I graduated high school. My siblings and I handled things at home differently, and my way of handling it was church, not realizing satan had a trap he was guiding me into, with eyes wide open yet blind to his devices.

Moving out

My family ended up moving to the south side of town, but I didn't want to move with them because of my job and because church would be on the other side of town. My family didn't like my decision, but they respected it. I ended up moving into an apartment building that was full of members of the church and becoming roommates with a teen mother who had two young children. My first night, I remember I cried so hard because I missed my family, but I was trying to be a grown-up. I did adjust over time and was determined to live for God. The neighborhood was infested with drug dealers and addicts – people would line up right outside of my second-floor bedroom window. I remember going out there to pray and pour oil right in those same spots where the people would line up when it was clear.

My passion was to help others

As years passed, the pastor and family would foster many children and adopt some as well. At that time, I was working as a bus attendant and a teacher assistant for special-needs children. I loved working to help others, as it is a passion of mine. I was then asked by the pastor if I could be a respite worker for a special-needs child they were about to bring home and hopefully adopt. This child had lots of medical issues, and they already had three other foster children. I was excited and said yes because I would not only be helping the people of God but also earning a third income. It was going to be a win, win, win as I got paid and helped.

Oh boy, was I nervous when I was going through training and seeing all the medical equipment to care for this child who looked so fragile. Nevertheless, I did learn how to take care of the child. During this time, one of the young ladies who lived with the pastor and was trained to care for the child ended up leaving. The pastor then called me and asked me to move in with them to care for her because they would be in and out of town quite a bit. After asking some questions, I ended up saying I would.

I began to grow fond of the child, but then they decided they didn't want a respite worker because it might take away some of their nursing hours. I was disappointed with their decision because now I wouldn't be getting paid. I would have to volunteer my time and not be compensated. I was told by the pastor that this is what the Lord had called me to do, so I just started taking care of the child as unto the Lord. After all, I wanted to be in the will of God and wanted to help God's people. We as Christians must get clear directions from God and not man on everything we plan to do. God talks to those who would listen, but many times, Christians don't even acknowledge him and go about our day just doing things by routine or according to what somebody else says we should do.

THE FIRST TIME I FELT LIKE I DIDN'T HAVE CONTROL OF MY LIFE

I recall living for God with all my might. Oh boy, I had the wrong perspective, because it's through Christ and grace that we are saved and not by works. Before moving in with the pastor, I had received a utility bill saying that I owed over a thousand dollars. I was puzzled because I had just paid the bill and it was less than 30 dollars, so I called the company to inquire about the bill, and they came out to check the meter and to investigate. As the utility company came out and went into the basement with two other individuals from the church who also lived in the building, I could see them talking among themselves. I didn't know what was being said, but I later received a phone call from the pastor yelling at me because now the entire building's gas was disconnected due to the investigation's findings.

I was confused and crying because I didn't know what I had done wrong. I was told by the pastor that it was my bill. I then proceeded to call the utility company, and they explained that the entire building's gas was connected to my apartment line, and that is why I received the bill. I only received an apology when I got a thousand-dollar check from the utility company after moving in with the pastor and her family – and gave her the entire check. The truth will always come out no matter how long it takes. We as believers should trust the process even when we don't understand; however, we shouldn't be ignorant but cautious and aware while wearing the whole armor.

Another time I felt like I didn't have control of my life is when I had plans to go to Mississippi. I was so excited to be going – they were going to have a shut-in, and I wanted to receive more from God. But then I was told that I couldn't go to the shut-in because I had to babysit a child of one of the members. I was upset and expressed my feelings to another church member, only to receive a phone call from the pastor later, as the individual had told the pastor what I had said. I was then rebuked in front of others, as the pastor had others around her when she called me. I did not attend the shut-in but spent the night crying instead. At that point, I began to be muted.

Control starts gradually

From the pulpit it would be said, " open rebuke is good for the soul", but going against another individual's will is witchcraft. One thing I have realized is that control starts in a very small way, gradually increasing when it's not properly addressed. Now, the individual feels and notices the abuse or control in the beginning, but many ignore it and think it will change. But change can't come until you speak up. I can recall noticing the change, but being unaware of what was taking place. I was with a group, and I began to tell them that I didn't know who I was. They all started laughing and saying jokes. I was for real, though, because I had really started losing my identity not only in Christ but as a human being. I had started doing things I thought were to please the Lord but were actually giving up my will to join other people's wills.

There are no two people exactly alike in the world. Even identical twins have different fingerprints. Twins can look alike, wear matching outfits, may share similar likes and dislikes, and it can even be hard to tell who's who, but they are each uniquely different. They are designed originals; God designed each of them with an individual purpose, and even though they were in the same womb, they will still have to answer to God individually, just as it is with everyone that is born. That is how we are in the body of Christ. We all have different personalities, yet we are set apart within the body of Christ. The way I do things may be different from how another person may do it. However, if we are obedient to God, and we are seeking his will and plans for our lives, he will be glorified and not man.

It's a fact that five plus five equals ten, but other combinations of numbers can also equal ten. The most important point is to get to the goal of ten. In the same way, the most important point in our lives is to fulfill the purpose that God created us to accomplish. You may be an eight plus two, someone else may be a nine plus one, but reaching the appointed designation symbolizes all our goals. If we are obedient, our personalities can be useful for God's glory. Therefore, never let an individual dictate to you, but only let the Holy Spirit lead, guide, and direct you as it is done with the love of God and according to the word of God.

The Holy Spirit is our teacher and our guide, for he is the Spirit of truth. Never forget that we have an enemy that desires to kill, steal, and destroy you. He wants to sabotage the plan and purpose God has for your life. No one is off limits for satan to use. So, beware! For we will give an account to God and not to man.

You could witness an individual who appears to be moving by the power of God, but remember, their lives must line up with the word of God. They must operate in integrity; they must not be a deceiver. When you are sincerely seeking God with your whole heart, he will reveal to you, no matter how long it takes. The true identity and operations of the person who once seemed so powerful to you will now be revealed by the true light of God. *"For the gifts and calling of God are without repentance"* (Romans 11:29

KJV). Therefore, a person can still operate in gifts, but if their heart is not connected to God, they are imposters. These are the ones to whom he will say, "Depart from me, for I never knew you" (Matthew 7:21-23). They will be reciting all the great works they did, only to find out they were doing it for themselves and not for God. You see, our hearts must be pure, for only the pure in heart shall see God (Matthew 5:8).

– CHAPTER 3 –

Unleash Yourself

As I looked up the meaning of the word "leash," I found that the dictionary defines it as "a strap or cord for restraining and guiding a dog or other animal." God doesn't want us to be strained or bound by anything that keeps us from living life in abundance in Christ. You see, I was bound, but I thought I was free. Yes, I had room to move, but only by the parameters that were given to me, because I was on a leash – not physically, but spiritually, for everything that exists in this realm also exists in the spirit realm. We must ask for discernment so we can know what is happening within the spiritual realm.

I was held on a leash by mere words spoken over me. The longer I remained in that unknown condition, the tighter the collar attached to that leash got, until it was so unbearable that I felt like I was dying – and truly I was, both spiritually and naturally. The result of being on a leash was evident in my physical body. If you don't feel free, you are probably not. If you feel bound, you most likely are. If you feel trapped, there's a good possibility you are. You can't get free by yourself – someone else has to unleash you, and that someone else is God, for he is waiting for you to cry out to him and ask him to unleash you.

Who the Son sets free is free indeed according to the word of God (John 8:36), for once we accept Jesus as our Lord and Savior, we know that we were freed over 2000 years ago when Jesus gave his life for us. As I think about how Jesus suffered just so I could be free, it makes me appreciate how it was done just for me, as I personalize the action he took just for me. One thing about God, he will let you know things, especially when you spend that quality time with him. For he will first let you know about yourself – yes, I said yourself. It is often said, especially within groups for issues like addiction, that you must acknowledge that you need help before you can receive help. People can look at other people and see their downfall but fail to see themselves. In order to be unleashed or released from something that has you bound, you must recognize the problem regarding yourself and have an urgency to want to be free.

THE DREAM

I had a dream that there was a dog chained to a wall outside of a building. As the dog kept barking and leaping forward, he was not able to go far because of the chain.

Suddenly, the dream switched, and it was me chained to a wall with a leash around my neck, only able to move as far as the chain would allow. As the dream continued, I was no longer chained to the wall, but the leash collar was still around my neck, and I stayed within those parameters that the leash had me in. I still had the mindset that I couldn't move any further than where the chain had me restricted. In the dream, I also heard God say, "Unleash yourself!" I then woke up repeating this to myself. God began to show me that he had set me free, yet my mindset was still in bondage, as I was living in a state of being chained even though the chain no longer existed. As long as you are restricted to a leash, someone else has control of the leash by guiding and directing your life, and you are not even aware of it. They can tell you how far you can go even without words. They can tell you if you are allowed to go by the tightness of the leash. They are in control, and you gave them that control, so now it's up to you to take the control back. It's a delicate situation, but it can be done by the power of God.

Many Christians are living in a mindset that is contrary to what God says we are. We do not have to live in bondage, for Christ has paid the price on Calvary. We don't have to be restrained, for freedom is being able to move and live free in Christ. Satan does not want us to know who we are, nor does he want us to know our rights in Christ. For as we recognize who we are, our identity, and our royal family background, that's when we stand up knowing that we are free, regardless of what is seen.

I knew what the word of God said, but I was still bound. I wasn't free mentally, as I didn't take God's word just as he said it. I've heard that it all starts within the mind. One thing I know for sure is that satan likes to play mind games, and many submit, thinking it's them and not discerning the tactics of the enemy. A lot of times, we are bound due to familiarity. God wants us to step out in faith, for he wants to do a new thing within us, and most times, a new thing can be uncomfortable. Trusting and believing in Christ must involve total dependence upon Christ, knowing you can't do anything without him.

I have a question for you: What are the leashes that are around your neck? What has you bound or in fear? Maybe it's a loved one, or the concern of being uncomfortable. Or maybe you were like me, fearful of what others thought, especially among the church leadership.

The church is supposed to be a safe haven, but all kinds of people come to church, and they should. It's just that the true believers need to be aware of their surroundings and the people who come into the building. They need to be aware that they are surrounded by saints and aints. Many in the church leave the way they came in. They refuse treatment from the Holy Spirit, who is the true physician. He doesn't just heal but makes you whole. But they must consent to the treatment by agreeing with the word of God. Many who come into the church building have no idea what the word of God says. Church people always say, "I wonder what God's will for me is," but if they would just read and study the word of God, they would find the will of God, because his word is his will.

A hospital is for the sick, and the physician treats all types of illness. However, before one can be treated, they must first consent to be treated, and if not, they leave the same way they came, untreated. Many are leaving the church worse than they came in. With a sincere heart, God will meet you where you are, for there is no condemnation in Christ Jesus. God wants you free in the mind, free in the spirit, and free to live. Christ unleashed you when he died on the cross. You are not trying to be free, because you are already free. Therefore, the people of God must guard their thoughts and meditate on the word of God, knowing that God's word is true and every thought that doesn't line up with the word of God is a lie. So, watch your thoughts along with your words that can produce life, bondage, and death.

– CHAPTER 4 –

False Appearances

Anything that is false represents something that is not the original. It can even present something that is like what is authentic, yet is not the real thing. The word of God even tells us that satan can present himself as an angel of light, for wolves would try to mingle themselves among the sheep to see who they can devour. God will separate the wheat from the tares as they grow together. Many will try to deceive you, but know that God has a way of escape that has already been done, as long as we trust him in everything, knowing that he is our deliver.

You must know who you are surrounding yourself with in your conversation, activities, and telling your business. I found that it is easy for the enemy to befriend someone who doesn't know where he or she stands with God. You can go to church all your life, but if you don't know the Lord or have an intimate relationship with him, the enemy will try to deceive you. Now, I'm not saying that you aren't living for God with all you have within you. What I am saying is that the enemy has studied you since your birth and knows the weakest points within your life, and he aims towards those spots by using people and circumstances.

A place of worship is supposed to be a place of safety, as so many would think, but we must realize that those who go to church or call themselves leaders within the church building are not always of God. Like I said before, many are out there being deceptive and being used by satan. Know that God is our protector, and we must have on the armor of God. I can recall myself saying, "God knows my heart." Well, that is true, but you have been studied, and obstacles have been placed to block you from completing your assignment. Not everyone who seems genuine actually is. Nevertheless, we are overcomers in Christ, and nothing will stop us from completing our assignment that we are supposed to display here on earth as our declaration. The body of Christ must wake up and have discernment about what is really happening even within religious organizations. Many false appearances are displayed within what many consider a church. This is because people are taking their pastors' and ministers' word instead of getting the word of God for themselves.

Now, God has given us pastors after his own heart, but we must not put our trust in religion but in Christ. What I have found is that many are not teaching the word of God but are applying their own interpretation by taking the word of God out of context. Paul said to follow him as he follows Christ. The key word is "following Christ" – how are they following Christ? We can't just talk this Kingdom language; we must display the characteristics of Christ. The word of God tells us that it's the little foxes that destroy the vine (Song of Solomon 2:15). This reminds me of how we think no one sees the little things, but God sees all. Yes, someone can preach, teach, and even cast out devils, but also use manipulation, control, and deceit and think it is all right, for their own accomplishments are the little foxes that destroy many vines due to selfishness and pride. Just make sure you are not associated with false appearances.

Truth and knowledge that is applied avoids deception. We must not look at the outward appearance, but view a person's actions, character, and motives. People can tell you anything, but over time, the truth will display itself. God will not have his people ignorant of anything if they seek his face. There are many religious theories out there today, and society in today's world incorporates many things that are contrary to the Kingdom. I believe this is because we are coming closer to the return of Christ with every second.

OPINIONS

People give their opinion or what they believe the scriptures are saying instead of going strictly by the word of God.

God doesn't need our opinion about anything, for his word stands regardless of your opinions or idealist thinking about what you believe. Not only is God's word true, but it will not and cannot be altered to fit man's views. You can disagree, but disagreeing doesn't change the word of God. I had to relearn things that were taught in the church as I judged others when they said something different from what I had been taught. God had to introduce me to a new set of people whose mindset was on the things of God and who gave me a greater hunger for the truth. One thing I realized is that you must be careful about who you listen to, because not everything that sounds good is always correct. The word of God must be approached as Truth, no matter what facts may represent. I once heard that facts can change, but truth remains the same. Christ is Truth, and he changes not.

– CHAPTER 5 –

Learning to Walk in Wholeness through Faith

The word of God tells us that Christ has come so that we can have abundant life in him, and wholeness can only be complete in him. An individual can try on their own to become whole but will fail without having Christ as the foundation. According to the dictionary, wholeness is "a state of being complete or being unbroken / undamaged." When one realizes they are whole, their perception changes concerning themselves, as they are renewed and put their confidence in Christ. I first had to realize that I needed help for me to accept wholeness. Oh boy, was it hard to face the facts, but the only way to deliverance was accepting truth, even during the pain – the pain that made me condemn myself for allowing things to take place, the pain of thinking of what others may say even if they didn't say anything. What a way to live, being in fear and believing the lie that first starts within the mind. Now that I look back, my faith was in what others thought, said, and believed in instead of what God said about who I was in him. Over the last few years, I have had to literally redirect my thought process by not only getting into the word of God but surrounding myself with like-minded individuals who had a hunger for God. Who you associate yourself with is important.

Self-discovery

As I was rediscovering myself, I was faced with lots of challenges that seemed to come one after another. I first found myself having surgery on my tonsils, then to fix a deviated septum, and the doctors saw on the CAT scan that the roots of my wisdom teeth were in my sinuses, so surgery on my sinuses was needed as well. Oh boy, that was that painful.

God impressed upon me to attend a Christian business college. I am so glad I followed the leading of the Holy Ghost. Attending the business college was like a lifeline thrown out for me while I was dealing with depression and suicidal thoughts. We had chapel every morning before class, and it seemed like the ministers were always on point, for you knew that the Holy Spirit was speaking through them. I began to grow in faith as the word of God began to come alive for me. I also started listening to different ministers on YouTube and learning new things that I had never known even though I had been attending church all my life.

As I meditated on what I read and roots of faith began to form, I started to declare God's word and speak it out of my mouth. There were many times I had prayed, crying about the problem and asking God to deliver me, but never actually declaring the word. I also did a lot of praying in silence, not knowing at that time that you have to say something verbally. God had me in the right place at the right time. We may not know exactly what God has in store for us, but his plans present the best outcome if we just trust him.

Some of my classmates and I began to not only discuss the class work but also make each other accountable for the words that were spoken out of our mouths. I recall saying something negative concerning myself, and they would say, "Take that back! We will not say anything that disagrees with God's word." We would even discuss the word and read books concerning the correct way to pray. All of this was new to me because I realized I had been praying the wrong way for most of my life. Many of us was taught the traditional way to pray, but not what the word of God says about how to pray. Little did I know at that time that what I was learning would need to be applied within the next few months. God has a way of preparing us.

Meanwhile, within a few months, I started having difficulty speaking, but it would always come back within a few minutes. At first, I didn't disclose what I was experiencing to anyone. However, after it happened a second time, I did tell my mom, and she told me that I need to call the doctor right away. I did exactly that, following her instructions. The doctor was on vacation, and the nurse instructed me to go to the emergency room. My response was that I didn't want to go because Covid-19 had just started and the emergency rooms were filled. She then said, "You need to go."

I went to the hospital, and I was feeling fine with no symptoms of anything going on, as I told the nurse before she instructed me to go. While I sat there waiting to be seen by a doctor, they decided to do lab work and a CAT scan with and without dye. The doctor came to speak with me, asking me if I was dealing with anxiety due to everything going on with people dying from the coronavirus, and I said no. He told me that they found nothing on the CAT scan. I told him that I knew what I was experiencing, but I didn't have those symptoms now and it had only happened a few times. He then decided to redo the CAT scan and go a little further down my neck this time.

Afterwards, the same doctor came back into the room I was in and told me something totally different than before. He said he saw that I had had several mini strokes, and I also had very little blood flow going to the right side of my brain. I was then told that the neurologist and surgeon would have to be contacted and I must see them as soon as possible. Of course, my first instinct was to begin to cry and call my mom. I later contacted the dean of the business school, and he prayed and got an intercessor from the church to call me. I didn't contact many people to pray because I didn't want everyone praying for me. You may ask me, "Why is that?" As I began to read and study the word of God, I saw that it says that by his stripes we were healed, not "going to be healed" or "praying for a healing." I had learned that everything that was done for me, including healing, was done on Calvary. I just wanted to thank God for my healing. I also began to recognize that people praying would pray in doubt, and with my life on the line, I couldn't take that chance with prayers that didn't even hit the ceiling.

I began to put on sermons by Kenneth Hagin and others as well. I recall one of his sermons where he talked about how one side of his face was drooped as if he were having a stroke. He stated that he went to church and people kept saying something about his face. In response, he began to say that he was healed. He stated that people would tell him, "You said you were healed, but your face still looks the same." No matter what they said, he would still say he was healed. As I was listening to him on YouTube, hearing his testimony made me realize all the more that no matter what is seen, felt, or said, we must still declare the word of God.

Meanwhile, the symptoms were starting to come more frequently, especially after the doctor told me what he had seen. I just kept confessing what the word of God said and took communion daily. I was already healed according to the word, so no matter what the symptoms tried to tell my flesh, I was still standing on the word of God. I had to go and take a MRI and a MRA, and both confirmed what the emergency room doctor had said, but I still had to line my faith up with the word of God, telling the enemy that while what they saw was a fact, it wasn't the truth. For I am still confessing and believing the word of God. I know it doesn't seem logical to some, but one thing I have discovered is that God works outside of logic so that no one else can get the glory.

SURGERY

I had gone to get a second opinion from another doctor, and he confirmed what the other doctor had said. However, he wanted to do an angiogram, which showed no blood flow to the right side of the brain. He also stated that this had to have happened within the last seven years. I really begin to give God the praise as I was putting into place what I had been learning. You might ask why, but I realized that I was still able to function and do things that I shouldn't be doing. It was God working all the time.

The doctors said we needed to schedule this operation as soon as possible. However, I told him that I was in school and would graduate in January. I expressed to the doctor that I wanted to finish school first. He explained to me that I was putting myself at risk, but it was my choice. I felt that God had kept me all that time, so he would continue to keep me. God did just that, and I give him all the honor, glory, and praise.

On February 11, 2021, I went in to have brain surgery, making it to the hospital at 5 a.m. that day not in fear but in faith. I felt as though God had a greater plan that I truly did not understand, and I yet trusted him in the process. Family couldn't stay due to Covid, so I had to be there all alone. However, I was never alone, for my Savior was there with me all the time. As I was preparing by putting on the hospital gown and getting the IV put in place, the team of doctors and nurses came in to talk to me concerning what was going to take place. One doctor came in to tell me that she oversaw a team they had for me (the ICU team). She explained that they were going to try to wake me up only one time, and if I didn't wake up, they would keep me sedated with the tube still in me for seven days. I said to myself that I was going to wake up the first time. One thing I can say is that although I was about to go into brain surgery – which the doctor expected to last for 23 hours – I was not afraid, for I had the word of God built up within me.

PRAISE PARTY

As a matter of fact, the day before surgery, I was just having a praise party, thanking God while cleaning and baking a cake for my niece whose birthday was the same day of the surgery. She was surprised that I was able to still make her cake knowing what I was going through, but I refused to give the enemy any room. For *"in everything give thanks"* (1 Thessalonians 5:18 NKJV).

SURGERY OVER

I said I would wake up from surgery on the first try, and I did. The doctors were so pleased of the outcome, and I didn't have to go to ICU but a step up, and the surgery took 10 hours instead of 23. God is so good, and he has us covered as we trust and believe in him. I remember being in a lot of pain, but God. As I'm writing this, I can't help but to think about how it has been almost a year since this day.

In the hospital, I tried to practice speaking only positive things, even though negative voices would try to enter my thoughts. You see, satan wanted me to reflect on "Why me?" I prayed, I believed, but if you look at it, I was thinking "I" all the time. That is how the enemy tries to deceive us – by putting thoughts in our head. He didn't once say "God performed a miracle," "God has a purpose and plan," or "This will be a great testimony."

I can recall looking in the mirror for the first time a week after the surgery. I wanted to cry as I saw my face so swollen. One eye was barely open, and the other one couldn't open at all. "My face!" is what I thought. But as I looked at myself sitting in that wheelchair, I could hear my friend saying, "Girl, you are gorgeous, and remember, do not say any words contrary to the word of God." I began to look at myself differently from that moment on. Whenever I would see myself in the mirror, I would say, "Girl, you look good, and you are gorgeous."

I remember having very little strength, and the doctor came in and wanted to talk to me. He said, "You are going to have to move and push yourself," because I couldn't even sit up on my own. He began to explain that if I didn't, I could die. That same evening, I begin to push while still trusting God. I pushed despite the pain and the way I felt. As I think about it now, God wants us to push regardless of our past, regardless of what it looks like, and regardless of what others say. But most of all, I wanted God to get the glory out of my life even in this situation. God begin to put some of the staff among me with the opportunity to witness to them. I told one nurse that God had a plan for her life and that he loved her, and she began to share some things with me. It was not about me but for God to be glorified.

Rehab

It was time to leave the hospital and go to rehab so I could learn to walk again. I refused to be defeated, so I pushed. I recall trying to spell the word "recognize" and not knowing how to spell it. Tears began to come. My speech therapist explained that it would come back, as it was like files in my brain that were everywhere and needed to be reorganized. Now that I look back, God was doing something supernaturally. It was like rewiring with a new mindset. God set me in a place to help others that I wouldn't have met if I had not been in that place. I started encouraging other patients who were down due to having a stroke or other injuries. We would be using walkers and I would say "You got this" or "You're doing a great job." One therapist would tell me, "That person hadn't smiled since they've been in here, and you were making them smile." I had some staff coming and talking to me about issues, and I was able to encourage them as well because of Christ. I was realizing all the more that it was a much bigger picture than I thought. We can only see a portion, but God knows the whole story. I once heard Myles Munroe say, Our "future is God's past". So why not trust God who knows your past, present, and future.

When I left rehab, I had to go stay with my parents because I still needed support physically. I began to go to day rehab, and walking with a walker was like a chore, but over time, God continued to show me his grace and love while still downloading into me. Four months later, I was allowed to go home. When I left day rehab, my speech therapist told me that when I came, my reasoning skill was less than 1%, but when I tested again before leaving day rehab, I tested above 100%. I give all praises to God. I had to meditate on the word of God and speak what the word said despite what the doctors said and how I felt. When we walk in faith, we must hear while believing what the word of God says, blocking out every other voice while standing and not detouring towards fear, doubt, and unbelief.

– CHAPTER 6 –

Standing Regardless of What Is Seen or Felt

Life itself can offer lots of opportunities. But as believers, we must be in tune with the Holy Spirit so that we don't miss what God is doing in that very moment. The enemy wants us as believers to concentrate on things that we see and the opinions of others to try to throw us off from fulfilling the perfect will of God. But the Holy Spirit is our guide, and allowing him to teach and direct us will prevent many delays and mishaps along the way. As I think about how Eve was set up in the garden of Eden, she knew that God said not to eat from the tree, yet listening to the serpent, she did eat. Just as she listened to the serpent, we must be careful not to listen to anyone who goes against the word of God. We can see that Adam also ate, causing them both to die spiritually. They were deceived by what they heard from the enemy, for it was a setup. Satan's tricks are not new, and he is always trying to set the people of God up. Don't be set up by logic. Don't be set up by believing lies.

I realize reality can seem to be so real due to everything being tangibly felt, heard, and seen – not only by us as individuals, but also by others we associate with, because they are like the witnesses that can become agreeable partners with our experiences. People who associate together have something in common, and that common ground makes them witnesses that can become agreeable partners. But what we see is not always the truth. I have heard a saying, "There are three sides to every story: your side, my side, and the truth." As believers, we must agree with the word of God, and that agreement will produce results that correspond to the will and word of God. And the three sides to that story are Jesus our Redeemer, who was the greatest sacrifice; the Holy Spirit our guide, who will teach and direct us in which way to go; and Yahweh, the One and ONLY true God. For God is all-knowing, his judgment is just, and his love is pure. God so loved us that he gave his only Son (John 3:16).

Being balanced

When we are standing, we must be balanced. If someone is not balanced, they will most likely fall, for standing requires trunk control and strength. I recall the physical therapist working with me on my balance, and she presented different activities to improve it. First, she would instruct me to go in between the balance beams, holding on with one hand. Then I gradually used just the tips of my fingers, and finally, I was able to complete an exercise without any assistance of holding on.

I realize we must also stand up in the Holy Spirit by trusting in God and having faith in him, for the word of God says that without faith, it is impossible to please him (Hebrews 11:6). As I used one hand, I was using faith to complete the exercise, and my faith gradually increased so that I eventually did not need to hold on to anything. We must balance ourselves with the word of God because the battle is in the mind. Whatever situation you are facing, the enemy is always there on his job trying to plant doubt, uncertainty, and discouragement. Therefore, we must be on our job to properly use the word of God to dismantle and take into captivity every thought that exalts itself against the knowledge of God (2 Corinthians 10:5). Just as I listened to the physical therapist, we must listen to the Holy Spirit to instruct us so we can stand firm on the word of God using the armor of God. By doing so, we walk in the victory that Jesus has already given us, for we are more than conquerors in Christ Jesus (Romans 8:37).

God gives us a NEW sense

Life within itself presents physical traits that focus on the outward appearance, registering our senses of taste, seeing, hearing, feeling, and smell. However, God gives us another sense when we accept him as our personal Savior, which is the Holy Spirit that we need to rely on daily in everything we do. Let me encourage you to rely on that sense more than any others. When you do, you will be relying on God and not yourself.

We must overcome what we see, what we hear, and what we feel, for satan tries to detour us from victory by making it appear as if our goal is impossible to reach by reflecting on natural circumstances. And if we are not careful, it will drown out the sense or the voice of the Holy Spirit, causing us to walk in carnality and in a state of defeat, when in reality, you are a VICTOR and not a victim. We are overcomers, the head, subduers, and more than conquerors in Christ Jesus. I did say "more than conquerors." A conqueror is someone who wins and overcomes. Just know that victory is already won.

In the word of God, Elisha prayed for God to allow eyes to be opened so the young man could see that there was more help with them in the battle than it was with the enemy. You see, the young man couldn't see in the spiritual realm until his eyes were open. Only then could he see that the mountain was full of horses and chariots of fire on behalf of them (2 Kings 6:16-17). Therefore, we as believers must stay in tune with the Holy Spirit by taking God's word for what it says, despite what our natural eyes see and what logic tells us is real. This journey comes with constantly learning how to walk in the supernatural. It must be practiced daily as we reflect on the word of God and not what surrounds us but who is with us.

We are Kingdom citizens who were born from heaven but came into this atmosphere to bring heaven to earth. Don't consider it strange when people think you are weird for believing in the supernatural and not in things that make much sense. I believe the world tries to contaminate or poison what we know as the truth by presenting ideas and systems that make up their facts according to their beliefs, which contradict the word of God.

Yes, pain will come, and so will doubt from time to time, but know that every symptom and appearance that doesn't line up with the word of God is not true, regardless of what is seen, felt, or heard. Many times, I didn't understand why a situation was taking place, and I started to reflect on what I was feeling. And to be honest, at that point, I was a participant in a pity party I helped organize by rehearsing what I felt was unfair. Little did I understand that God still had a plan that would make me stronger as I trusted him. By utilizing each day, taking it one day at a time, I am walking in the knowledge that I already have the victory in Christ. You also are a victor in Christ, and satan knows that also which is why he doesn't want you to know the authority you have in Christ.

– CHAPTER 7 –

FIGHTING WRONGFUL THINKING

Fighting is a battle that occurs to take someone under and causes them to submit to another as they surrender by force or cave in. Wrongful thinking first starts within the mind.

The word of God tells us that we can experience peace that passes all understanding while guarding our mind and heart (Philippians 4:6). Our thoughts bring about outcomes that will manifest due to what we dwell upon. That is why we must cast down every thought that does not line up with the word of God. Those thoughts come from the enemy, even if he has to use others to plant seeds of negativity and encourage you to water them by agreeing, accepting, and dwelling on it.

Awareness

We must be aware of people in authority or in positions over us because these are the people that you trust, but they too can be used by the enemy to plant those seeds of negative thoughts. One thing I have realized is that thoughts can be suggestions, and we must be careful to guard our eye and ear gates. If we dwell upon a negative thought, it takes root and can get within our hearts, causing us to believe something is true when it is a lie. After entering within the heart, those thoughts will control your actions or come out in the form of sickness. The word of God tells us to guard our heart with all diligence (Proverbs 4:23). It all starts within the mind; nevertheless, know that God's word is the only truth.

Back when I was caring for a child in my pastor's home, I found myself dwelling upon the negative, questioning my feelings and desires as I was abruptly brought back to the reality of what the people in authority said I was going to do. I felt like I was caught in a web with no way of escape, and everything I tried to do was not good enough. Many times, we as believers don't quite understand the process of what we are going through. All we see is the negative. But even though we can't see, we must know through faith that we are overcomers. No, I didn't understand, as I gave up everything, even my finances and my time, and I couldn't see family unless I let them know and was granted permission to do so.

I was working two jobs, and yet I had to come home to care for a special-needs child for four hours, and then many times throughout the night – there was no nurse at night, so I had to stay up to feed her through a g-tube (feeding tube), do her respiratory therapy, and attend to other medical treatment that was required for her care. I loved the child, and because of my love, I endured regardless of feeling overwhelmed and like things weren't fair, as I was her main caregiver even though she had adoptive parents. I was always told that this was my job from God. There were many times I couldn't go to family gatherings due to being told I couldn't go or having to be back by 6 p.m. when the nurse got off work.

I didn't want to complain because it was a sin. Yet in my mind, I questioned everything. Why did I have to give them my whole check and only be allowed two hundred dollars a month to live on? Why couldn't I go out of town like everyone else but have to stay to babysit two special-needs individuals and three dogs? Why couldn't I spend time with my family more? Why did I have to ask for permission for just about everything I did? I felt like a little girl in a grown woman's body. Satan presented suggestions and lies and had me questioning the actions that I allowed.

Fighting Wrongful Thinking

All actions occur by first thinking about them. This can happen through a thought or a suggestion, but either way, it is thought about and then followed through with an action. Every time a thought takes place or an image form, if we aren't careful, actions will follow. God gives us a way to escape any temptation from a thought, but he never takes our free will to do so.

According to a study from the University of California, Irvine, "it takes an average of 23 minutes and 15 seconds to get back to the task" when regrouping thoughts. So, therefore, we must guard what we are thinking and dwelling upon. Negative thinking can cause a lapse in the important things that can be accomplished, and we must weed out the negative things by quoting the word of God. Satan tries to detour the believer, and if he can't detour you, he wants to slow you down, cause you to reconsider and reprocess, and hinder as much as possible of your God-given assignment.

Meanwhile, "the average person has about 48.6 thoughts per minute, according to the Laboratory of Neuro Imaging at the University of Southern California. That adds up to a total of 70,000 thoughts per day." This statement shows that we are always thinking. But what are you thinking about? The word of God tells us to think on things that are lovely, pure, and of good report (Philippians 4:8). Just know that the adversary is always looking for a way to distract, suggest, and offer things that lead to destruction.

We must all learn to guard our thoughts and cast down every thought that's not like God. Wrongful thinking can be damaging and can take a longer time to come back to reality once an individual discovers the truth.

I believe that wrongful thinking can also cause sickness, depression, anxiety, and low self-esteem. As negative thinking plagued my thoughts, I became depressed and spent most of my time having a pity party and playing the victim. I now praise our Lord and Savior, for I am not a victim but a victor in Christ Jesus. I give him all the glory for delivering me and bringing me out. I had anxiety about what others thought, as I was always trying to please them. It was even to the point that I would pray for me to have a good day at home and ask God to allow me to do and say the right things before entering the house.

The spirit of fear had a stronghold and root within me. I became so sick that I was diagnosed with Crohn's and had to have several surgeries. Right before one surgery, I remember one doctor came in my room and told me that I needed to start thinking positive and that would help the condition I was in at that point. I just looked at the doctor thinking, "You don't understand," as I had hidden all my feelings on the inside and they were radiating in my body physically, though I didn't realize it at the time. The doctor was telling me to start thinking positive and didn't confess Christ, yet I was a believer who should have known this, but I was deep in bondage with shackles within the spiritual realm. This also caused me to accept the current lifestyle, yet I was still hoping for a change, not realizing at the time that I had to change my mind set to become free.

Wrongful thinking violates the word of God. Any type of negative thinking doesn't line up with who God is and what God says. A negative mindset consists of a repetitive way of thinking which is not pleasant and does not display hope. Once we become believers, we must not just read the word of God, but meditate on the scriptures and confess what the word says. I have found that I must practice this daily, for the adversary is always not only looking for our words in the negative things we say about ourselves but also trying to place images through our thinking to get us to relate, accept, and display them. We are human and living in this fleshly body with thoughts that will come on a constant basis but knowing who we are in Christ makes all the difference.

There are many churches out there. I have seen multiple churches just within the same block. However, there are many believers who still do not know who they are in Christ. I believe that many are teaching what to do and what not to do instead of teaching who they believe they are in Christ and the authority they have as believers. How can you fight with a negative mindset if you don't know who you are and yet are condemned within the law? To walk in true freedom, it first starts in the mind. By changing our way of thinking, it changes our behavior as well. Our actions display a different aura that results in a positive outcome.

– CHAPTER 8 –

Recognizing the Enemy

To recognize an enemy, one must first know who their enemy is. An enemy is a foe trying to do you harm in some sort of way. The word of God tells us that the enemy comes to kill, steal, and destroy. Satan is a deceiver: he seduces mankind to sin or into a false doctrine, blinding them with lies. An enemy can pretend to be an ally, only for you to discover later that their motives were not in your best interest. For all things will come to the light eventually, no matter how long it takes. Nevertheless, we can also be an enemy to ourselves just through wrongful thinking about ourselves.

Who are you listening to? Is it that lie that the enemy is trying to suggest? Is it that dream-killer that discourages you from believing in what you want out of life? Is it a situation that desires to take your joy?

First, our eyes must be opened to recognize the enemy. Someone with blind or blurred vision can't see clearly regarding their surroundings, which affects their environment. The enemy seeks to blind us by presenting false perceptions. I know that I didn't see the enemy for who he truly was. I was only focusing in on tunnel vision, which is, according to Wikipedia, "the loss of peripheral vision with retention of central vision, resulting in a constricted circular tunnel-like field of vision." I was unable to see what was on the side of me and had a blind spot that kept me from seeing what was approaching.

I was so focused on making sure everybody else's life was good that I ignored my wellbeing both mentally and physically, as well as the desires that I wanted to accomplish to make a difference in life. I didn't care who you were – I even would have defended and protected those who were actually doing harm to me. I was blind and did not really know who the enemy was, so I thought I was supposed to go through these things for God. I even rejected those who could actually see the enemy for who he was. It was only when I was no longer in that environment that I truly saw the damage that had been done, which I had not been able to see in its entirely. When you are in something, you cannot see the reality of the situation. Only when you step back can you truly see, and even then, things are not completely revealed. I suffered with accepting the truth and yet trying to defend those who were leaders over me. Only to realize later that truth is freedom.

So, how are we going to fight the enemy once we recognize who he is? What are you going to do about it? Are you going to wallow in what should have been and what was? First, the enemy can't be fought in a natural sense, for we are in a spiritual battle that requires a unique armor designed for spiritual warfare. We have one effective weapon in fighting the enemy: the word of God. The enemy wants us to use our feelings or what we see instead of using the word of God. I found myself not really praying or speaking the word of God, but just crying many days. Yes, God bottles our tears up, but crying is not a weapon, for it does not produces an effective result in warfare. Even Jesus had to use the word of God against the enemy, for he stated what was written, and therefore, we must also use what has been written.

Pity party

Wallowing in our feelings produces a delay, doubt, self-pity, and unbelief, but no results in fighting the enemy. In actuality, it gives the adversary a foothold to try to keep you in the same state of thinking. I can recall being in the hospital having a pity party. I had asked God to take me on the operating table, and as I was crying, I heard a still voice that said, "You can't choose your testimony." I then asked God to forgive me and shut my mouth. I believe God will meet you wherever you are if you will allow him to.

God has given us the authority, and life and death is in the power of our tongue.

We must know that we are conquerors when we have Christ. If you do not know who you are, the enemy will tell you who you are not.

Many times, we sense something that may feel a little awkward, but most of the time, we ignore or disregard those feelings. We will even say to ourselves that something just isn't right or there's a suggestion that we just feel uncomfortable with, but we do it anyway. Red flag actions by individuals are warnings that make us question motives. Therefore, we must make sure we are truly hearing God, not flesh or suggestions. I believe that we as humans can get so caught up with this realm, focusing on what we see in the natural, that we do not always think of the spiritual realm, which is more real than this one.

– CHAPTER 9 –

Walking in Freedom and Free from Religion

To walk in freedom is an experience no man can describe without having once been in bondage. I have learned that many have an opinion about what someone else should do when they themselves wouldn't know what to do if they were in that person's shoes. Freedom has the ability to loose chains that once had you bound. Freedom is when fear no longer reigns over you. When one does not experience freedom, it's like running on a wheel, like a hamster going nowhere – the hamster is running and the wheel is going around, and yet no progress is being made. I personally found myself running, striving, and doing all I could to live up to man's conditions, and yet being tired, discouraged, irritated, and unfulfilled.

When you look at religion, it is a belief in a supreme God with a system of faith and the way one worships. Therefore, man has turned religion into a system that corresponds with what they think rather than what God says, which has caused religion to become distorted. To be honest with you, when you truly worship God, it becomes a relationship. This relationship develops as one communes with God and understands his unconditional love just for them. After all, that is why we were created, to commune with God, just like Adam and Eve did in the garden before the Fall. God desires to commune with you, he is not mad at you, and he is waiting for you to come to him with a sincere heart. You will no longer have to accept the feeling that good things will never happen for you.

SLAVERY

I contemplated about my ancestors and how they endured slavery – bound by their masters, bound by their performance, and bound by how they looked. Many slaves died for freedom, while many stayed and suffered and endured. Why did some never fight for their freedom, but want it deeply? Why did others take that chance knowing it was possible for them to perish along the way? They all saw the lynching, they all heard the dogs, they all saw the guns and experienced the threat of them being fired. Yet some took a chance and others didn't. I even think of Harriet Tubman and how she risked her life because she wanted her people to be free from slavery and to experience what freedom felt like. Chains, rope, whips, beatings, dogs, rape – the slaves knew what each meant and yet felt powerless in the midst of it.

They first had to know and recognize the position they were in. They had to learn what slavery entails. It was like there were two types of slaves. One set of slaves was content not to see themselves free, for they couldn't see beyond where they were at, while the other set of slaves had a vision of where they saw themselves as freed people. As Proverbs 29:18 (KJV) says, *"Where there is no vision, the people perish."*

The open door represents the freedom one can have. Yet fear of what is on the other side can keep you in bondage due to the unknown. Faith is the key, but love unlocks the door. For Christ is the door, and because of him, we freely have a choice to walk therein. Many Christians are yet in bondage even though they have accepted Jesus as Savior. They are free because whatever needs to be done is already done due to Calvary, but many are still living in bondage because their dependency is upon man and not Christ. For many are raped in the spirit, not naturally, but violated as the enemy has taken everything. Taking your time, for time is precious and you can never get that back. It is important to use our time with purpose. Taking your energy, trying to make you tired so you don't have the strength to do the things God has called you to do. Taking your finances by sowing in soil that won't produce and using manipulation to keep you in a place of uncertainty.

I realize that walking in freedom is when you can truly see and admit that you need to be free. I remember the day my freedom had come physically, but mentally I was yet bound. I had left a church that I had attended for over 20 years. They were like family, and I was accustomed to their ways and beliefs. I knew God had called me for more and I wouldn't be able to fulfill the will of God there. Yet I lived in fear, wondering what leadership would say and how they might rebuke me in front of others. It was always said that open rebuke was good for the soul, but it produced fear, so even when I knew I was right I did not say anything.

God does not want us to live in bondage or fear. I truly did not see how bound I was until I left, and the longer I was gone, the more I could see the bondage I was in, because when you are there, you are blinded to the devices of the enemy. I found out that you truly can't see when you are close up to something. Only when you get to a certain distance can you truly see. It's like a picture – the individual getting their picture taken can't see what the photographer sees until they are able to see the picture afterwards.

You must love yourself enough to want to be free, even if it means disappointing the next person. Your wellbeing and happiness are up to you, and therefore, you have to take initiative in order to be free. Finally becoming free was not an easy journey for me, but it was necessary. Freedom brings joy and a sense of being able to move without the mental chains that had held me down for years, for freedom consists of having choices, not being bound, or restrained. Freedom means being free of bondage and not being under any type of influence of other people and things, with no one that will control my life. It means giving God full access, without pressure from others but truly on my own. In order to know freedom, one must first know bondage. How good it feels to be relieved of the stress and pressure that comes with bondage. Bondage is like slavery or a prison that has only one way out, with a constant whip on one's back, as one cries out in despair, only silently in fear.

– CHAPTER 10 –

Delicate Yet Unbreakable

Tough situations that we all face are just a part of this life we live here on earth. We all have something we have dealt with, and no one is exempt unless they have died and are in the presence of the Lord. No matter what has happened, it has presented an experience that is unforgettable but has also shaped your life, your perception, how you interact with others, and your outlook on things that you correspond with on a daily basis. Those experiences do not have to break you, but they can make you stronger while living out a delicate situation.

After leaving the church and the pastor's home I can recall crying and telling my mom I didn't understand how I allowed things to happen. I felt like it was my fault because I didn't see what was really going on. She reminded me of something God gave her concerning me. She stated that God had shown her an expensive chain that was worth a lot of money. The chain was all knotted up, and it was so tangled that it looked impossible to detangle without breaking it if not handled carefully. She began to explain that I was that chain. God was setting me free even in the most delicate season of my life. That chain had so much worth, and God still had use for it. But we must allow God to detangle us by relaxing in his care, for he knows what to do and how to do it. We may not understand, but we must trust him so that we don't break. Sometimes when we are being detangled, it does not feel comfortable, but it is based upon our faith in God's word and not how we feel or see it, because God's word is the final authority.

There are times, in life, you may think that things are so bad that you are not worthy to be happy . The enemy will talk to you, whispering in your ear and making you feel as though you are worthless. At many times, his voice will get louder and louder, causing those feelings to intensify, whispering, "Don't nobody understand. God doesn't love you. You might just end it all." All these whispers are lies. He can make you feel all these ways: "No one cares, you are not worthy. Why even pray? Because he is not going to hear you anyway." Never forget, satan is a liar and everything he says is a lie. So, it's very important to know the truth of God's word and to know it for yourself. Satan wants to get you alone to present these thoughts, but know you have a Savior who wants to detangle you in your most delicate season. With Jesus' gentle touch, he will loosen and set you free from every knot, kink, hurt, insecurity, and pain. He will totally restore you and polish you with a shine so bright that no man can deny it and all will see the presence of God upon your life.

God will cause you to prosper in every area of your life. What was torn down, God can rebuild. It's no surprise that Jesus' occupation was to be a carpenter – he knows how to set the foundation, for he is the foundation. He knows the plan of the blueprint because he was there when the greatest architect of all designed the plans for your life. He knows what bricks to lay on the outside and the right interior design for the inside. The most important thing is to allow him to do the building. Remember, he is the expert, not you. God doesn't use the cheap material – he only uses the best, for he knows your worth even when you don't. We are worth so much that Jesus came to rescue us. You don't rescue something that is not worthy of being rescued. So, if Jesus knows our worth, so does satan, who tries to deceive you of your true worth and make you think you are nothing. In actuality, you are valuable to God.

I will be forever grateful for what God has detangled me from. God will send laborers across your path. I was blessed to have many laborers who were praying for me even when I didn't know they were praying. There was something going on within the spiritual realm, just like when Daniel prayed and it was heard immediately, but he didn't get an answer for twenty-one days because it was a spiritual warfare within the heavenlies that caused the delay. The delay didn't mean it was denied. So, whatever you think has been denied, I encourage you to continue to stand in faith trusting God, and whatever you do, please don't change your confession. We must agree with the word of God for it to come to pass. That is why our confessions must line up with the word of God.

God would put me on different individuals' hearts and have them interceding on my behalf. In my most vulnerable state, the enemy tried to destroy me. There were many times when I felt so low that I contemplated ending my own life, because I felt my life was passing me by while I was feeling unappreciated as I was doing all I knew to do. I was depressed about not even being able to make my own decisions as I submitted to what they wanted me to do. I was so overwhelmed with a lot of sleepless nights when a nurse did not come in to work. I was also ill, and I was told that I was exaggerating and must do what God sent me there for, which was to take care of the pastor's adopted special-needs children.

My mind was fighting a battle that I felt was impossible to win, but God said, "Not so – I got you." He saw my heart and knew that I desired to please him. I'm reminded of Jesus, who has prayed for us. For satan desires to sift us as wheat (Luke 22:31), but Jesus has already prayed that our faith does not fail. Praise God that his grace and mercy kept me. No matter what is going on in your life, God still has you on his mind. Just like God kept me, he is able to keep you too. If he has detangled me, he can detangle you, for there is no situation too hard for my God. Thank God I am free, untangled, and the enemy couldn't break me.

– CHAPTER 11 –

The Season Was Necessary

God's plan is that we experience different seasons in our lives. I believe that each season teaches us how to deal with the unexpected changes that occur in life. During each season, we learn to adjust to whatever season we are in and prepare accordingly. Depending on where you live in the world, each season brings about different temperatures and storms that suddenly change and sometimes catch you off guard where you might not be prepared. In some parts of the world, they don't get the same bitter cold, wind, and snow as others. You would hear some say, "I don't like to be cold, so I don't want to live in certain states," or "I don't like to be so hot, so I don't want to live in that state." But no matter where you live, you adjust to the season you are living in, and that season causes you to proceed with different actions.

Winter

In the winter, you most likely would wear a coat and clothing to keep you warm. If you don't wear the protective clothing, you could get frostbitten or even freeze to death. In the winter season, it gets darker faster. I even notice people cook differently during certain seasons as well. You may cook more homemade soups or chili during this time, and most people stay in the house more than they normally would if it was warmer outside. Some people like the snow as they go skiing, sledging, throwing snowballs, making snowmen, and ice skating. Even though it may be cold and snowing, it can still be enjoyable. However, some winters are harsher than others, and it can drop below zero.

When we are in the winter season in our lives, so is it in the spiritual within our lives. The winter season can be the toughest season someone can endure. My winter was enduring sickness as I was diagnosed with Crohn's disease. I had so much pain in my abdominal area. I remember barely walking and going to the doctor to see what was going on. The doctor examined me and said, "We need to get you to the hospital right away." There was so much infection in my intestines that the doctor said it was the size of a football. I didn't understand why all of this was happening to me. I was then told by the pastor that it was a big ball of sin. I cried, asking God, "What have I done wrong to deserve this?" All I did was go to work and come home to the pastor's house and take care of her special-needs children. I felt isolated, humiliated, and unable to share my true feelings because I had already committed some type of sin that I was not aware of, according to the pastor. I cried, telling God that I had given up my life to serve the pastor and her family, even putting them before my own family. I had many surgeries and was so depressed, not wanting to live, yet hiding it all within.

Even though I was sick, I was still required to take care of the pastor's special-needs children, as I was told that was why God sent me there and I had to pass the test. The child was supposed to receive twenty hours of nursing care daily, but much of the time, she did not receive the care from the agency because a nurse would call in for some apparent reason, so someone who was on the list in the home had to see to her and her medical needs. There were three people on the list, and I was the one who carried the entire load, even taking her to her doctor's appointments. When she went to the hospital to stay, I was the one who stayed and rarely went home to get a break. I recall staying twenty-one days with no relief. The doctors, nurses, and therapists knew me by name and would question me about why I never went home to take a break. I recall having to receive a port due to infusions that I had to take. The day of the surgery to receive the port, I had to go to the hospital to take care of her. I was told not to tell my family that I was at the hospital seeing to her. I immediately told the individual that I wouldn't tell my family where I was.

I am still talking about that winter season in your life where you may be living through a blizzard, feeling like you are in a cold and dark place with nowhere to turn. I had to learn how to do all of her respiratory therapy (which would cause her lungs to collapse if done incorrectly) and feedings through a tube in her stomach, give medication, and watch oxygen saturations, with no rest when a night nurse did not come in. I had to take off work when no nurse came in to work or when I had to take her to the doctor assisting the nurse. The doctor would ask me about her mom, but I would say that I was there to care for her because she was busy or out of town. Once I got too sick and the doctor told me that I couldn't go to work for a while, I still had to see to her, even after having many surgeries. I was even told that I was exaggerating when I told them I was in pain, and I was still made to care for the child. I would go in her room, lay my head on the foot of the bed, and cry.

Autumn

In the autumn season, we see the change even with the trees as the leaves begin to fall and change to beautiful colors. In the autumn, certain animals start to hibernate and prepare for the long winter months ahead. Plants also stop making food (producing). It is also the time to gather the harvest, and the day starts to get shorter. In the autumn of your life, things may not be severe as the winter, but it consists of challenges, disappointment, and having to adjust to some type of discomfort.

In the autumn season, people look at your outward appearance and see the beautiful colors like the leaves, but they don't know the story of why the leaves are falling. Everyone assumes everything is going well, and that's what you display, but deep inside, the blood is drying out. Everything in you is dry, and there is nothing being replaced within you. Don't they see you question yourself? Does God see you question?

My autumn consisted of learning to live without or learn to live with what I did not have. I had to learn to live off two hundred dollars a month, as I was required to give everything else to the pastor that came out of my disability check. They were also getting another check for me that was over twenty-three hundred a month, because I was granted a PA who is supposed to help you with different things around the home, but I was the one helping as they were taking. Yes, I did live there taking care of her children without pay. I had to budget, and when I ran out of the two hundred dollars, I was asked what I did with my money. Many times, I was hungry as they cooked in another part of the building or went out to dinner and didn't offer me anything. I would say to myself, "How did they forget about me?" when I couldn't go out because I was watching her special-needs children.

Autumns can be challenging learning to accept, adjust, and just wait and hope for change. I can recall having surgery, and the doctor gave me a prescription of antibiotics and pain meds. One of the other young ladies who lived in the home went to get my medicine. She kept checking on me, asking me if I was okay. Each time, I would say, "Yes, I will be okay." I thought she was really concerned, only to find out the real reason once I returned to church weeks later. As I was sitting there in church, the pastor said from the pulpit, "Tasha had surgery and I am not taking care of a drug addict." She then explained that she told the young lady who went to get my medicine from the store to exchange the pain medicine with some over-the-counter medication because she wasn't going to be taking care of an addict. I sat in church hurt as some laughed and others shook their heads.

Now, as I think back, that is why I probably got sicker, because I was only supposed to take pain medications the doctor gives when a person is diagnosed with Crohn's, as any other medicine can cause harm to the intestines. I still learned to adjust, with tears in my eyes, not knowing that God was taking every situation and making me a vessel to be used by him. I just kept being reminded that if you gave the prophet a glass of water, you would get an award. I would ask God, "When is it my turn?" I don't know your autumn season, but God does. God knows the intent of your heart and why you are doing what you are doing. I loved the child with special needs, but I had to put her in the hands of Jesus and love myself enough to know I needed to be refilled by him , for it was something man could not do for me.

Spring

Springtime is when things begin to bloom, and sometimes you can see all four seasons within it. You may experience it being chilly one day, and warm and rainy the next. It has even snowed here in Chicago within the spring season. You never know what the weather will be, so just be prepared to adjust and wear the appropriate clothing. When I think of my spiritual spring, I think of when my eyes began to open just as the flowers started to bloom. It became a time when, even though I was crying, I was also tired and wanted change. In the spring season, you must desire change and take steps towards change without knowing the disadvantages or advantages.

I remember clearly when my spring season had begun. The pastor, myself, and a few other members from the church were sitting on the porch, and they were talking about marriage. The pastor turned to me and asked if I still wanted to be married one day. I said yes. The church does not believe in dating, for according to the word of God, the Bible says husband and wife and not boyfriend and girlfriend, as it was explained to us in church. She said, " It was prophesied to you years ago that your husband was down south" and one of the members at the church said you missed out on getting married." I sat there in that seat on the porch saying the blood of Jesus under my breath. I was dedicated to serving my pastor and her family, but I desired a family of my own.

That same day, I was talking to my uncle, and I asked him about online dating. He said that he knew people who met online, and they have been married for over a decade. He then said that if I started talking to someone online, he would want to meet them. That very day, I made a profile, and I eventually did start talking to someone. It felt good to be able to talk to a male figure but knowing the church and its leadership would be against this. I begin to sneak and talk to him like I was a kid. He began to tell me that I was living in a bad situation and that I needed to leave and go stay with my parents. I felt like he was concerned about my situation.

One day, I was asked to go and put a car in my name for the pastor's teen granddaughter. I told them that I didn't want to do that because I didn't even have a car. I was then told that the pastor was looking into getting me a car, but that

I shouldn't say anything. I went with another individual who also lived in the home to get the granddaughter a brand-new car. While we were on the way back, I began to tell her that I was talking to someone because I was tired of sneaking. She then said that she was going to have to tell the pastor, but she would prefer if I told her. I told her that I didn't want to tell the pastor.

That Sunday morning, the pastor came back in town and asked to see me. When I went to see her, she had a set of license plates that I didn't sign for. She said, "I was going to give you this, but it looks like there's something you need to tell me." Of course, I knew that she knew about the guy I was talking to online. I cried as I was rebuked and said that I had a flesh problem. I was told to stop all communication. At first, I did, but then I thought about it and was like, "He didn't do anything to me, so why should I stop talking to him?" At church, it was mentioned from the pulpit. only my name was not mentioned. I was upset because she talked about her son getting one of the nurses pregnant and said that many people are doing things, but they just haven't been caught. I felt like I wasn't doing anything but talking on the phone, so to me, that was a slap in the face.

One evening, I received a phone call saying that my mom had fallen, and the ambulance was taking her to the hospital. I was in the room watching the pastor's special-needs child, and there were a lot of people in the part of the house where the pastor was. I was not allowed to go and see about my mom. Of course, the pastor prayed though. The next morning when the nurse came, I was allowed to leave to go check on my mom. The doctor said that she had bleeding on the brain, and they were not sure if she was going to live. Her face was all bruised and swollen. I stayed as long as I could, until my sister had to drop me off at the train station because I had to be back home to relieve the nurse at 6 p.m. every day. I had a curfew every day even though her parents were there.

When I got home, the pastor asked, "How was your mom?" I began to tell her about the bleeding on the brain. She then replied, "Do you know why that happened to your mom?" I said no. She said it was because of my sins and asked if I was still talking to that man. I didn't answer, because I was, and I did not want to lie. She began to sound just like the Pharisees in the Bible who said "Let it be on us and on our children " I began to think that my mom is not my child. My eyes were really opening. Did she not care about my mom? I wasn't allowed to go see her when it first happened and had to take a train to the hospital. It's now my fault about my mom? Why didn't she call my mom herself just to check on her and pray for her on the phone at least? All these questions I had. My aunt was on hospice, and I was told I couldn't go see her because the pastor's special-needs child was in the hospital and there wasn't anyone who could come and relieve me. I then asked why and was told that I could not pray for her anyway because I was in sin, so why do I want to go and see her? I was so hurt because my aunt and I had a relationship. You see, my spring consisted of a lot of seasons in one, but it only made me strong so that I could become who I am today. Yes, those times were painful, but my eyes were opening.

Summer

Summertime is the hottest season, and the daylight time is the longest and the sunrise is the earliest of all the other seasons. It is a time when children are mostly out of school, and many go on vacation to enjoy family time. Growing up, I heard the saying that there is light at the end of the tunnel. I consider my summer season as the time when I got free. I remember getting a call from my mom telling me that my dad had gone to the doctor, and they gave him some news that was not so good. I was instructed by my dad not to tell anyone. He only wanted his children to know and to trust God in faith with him. I agreed, but I wanted to go and see him.

That next morning, I got up and left the house once the nurse had arrived. While I was at the Metra train station going to my parents' home, I received a phone call. I was told that I needed to come and watch the pastor's twin grandbabies. I then told the person who called me that I was not at home because I was on my way to my mom's house. A few minutes later, I received a call from the pastor saying that I needed to tell her when I was leaving. She knew I was grown, but I was still supposed to tell her when I leave. She had to do a funeral and needed me to watch them. I was not asked; I was just told what I was going to do.

I began to tell her about my father, and she then started to tell me it was my fault, and I shouldn't allow my parents to suffer or die because of my sin. She even told me that I had a black heart. I cried, but I still went to see about my father. I was asked what was wrong with my dad and I told them that he didn't want us to say, and I was honoring his request. I was told that I am supposed to tell my pastor. I still chose to honor his request. I was then told that God had shown her that he had prostate cancer, which was not true, but I still honored his request.

I knew then that this was not of God. I told them that I had chosen to leave to go help my mom and father. I was told it was not God's will for me to leave, but I knew it was time. I had been going to see a Christian counselor without them knowing. I had mentioned to one of the young ladies there that I needed help and wanted counseling, only to get laughed at and told to just pray. My counselor told me that I was in an abusive relationship with the family, and I didn't see it like that at that time. But when you are close to the situation, you don't see clearly until you have been gone for a while. I was free in body but not free mentally and emotionally. I had to receive deliverance in many areas of my life, but God is faithful and won't leave you hanging on by a thread. Each one of these seasons helped me become the woman I am today, and I have learned that our toughest and most unbearable season produces pressure that makes us into gems.

NO LONGER HIDDEN

I am no longer hidden, and I am now living out the purpose God has for my life. Now I can see that I am supposed to help others become free, and if I didn't experience those seasons, I wouldn't be here to tell my story of being free. I no longer have to hide who I am, because I now know who I am in Christ and the purpose he has for my life. God has a plan that will outweigh all the pain. You may be hidden, but God will bring you forth to declare and tell the world that Christ is the only way. Freedom doesn't exist when one is hidden; it exists once God sets you up front so the world can see what he has done for you and the prosperity he has provided to you. Just know you are not alone, and the fight has already been won. The pressure you may be experiencing is the gem you are becoming. God has the master plan, and he will use you to be a precious gem to twinkle into someone else's dark life.

You may feel like you are in a broken place, scattered with no hope. But the power of God can and will reshape, remake, and redirect you by making you whole in Christ. Reach beyond your break and get a grip on the promises of God. For he cannot lie and cannot reject his own word. Nothing is impossible; just continue to have faith, for wholeness is the designer's plan for your life.

REFERENCES

Muse, T. (2020). This is Nuts: It Takes Nearly 30 Minutes to Refocus After You Get Distracted. *Stacey Lastoe.*

Reference. (2020). How Many Thoughts Do We Have Per Minute? *Staff Writer.*

www.ingramcontent.com/pod-product-compliance
Lightning Source LLC
Chambersburg PA
CBHW071200090426
42736CB00012B/2399